Piercing Horizons

IN SEARCH OF NEW FRONTIERS

JURI SHARMA

BLUEROSE PUBLISHERS

India | U.K.

For permissions requests or inquiries regarding this publication, please contact:

BLUEROSE PUBLISHERS
www.BlueRoseONE.com
info@bluerosepublishers.com
+91 8882 898 898
+4407342408967

ISBN: 978-93-5819-128-8

Cover design: Tahira
Typesetting: Tanya Raj Upadhyay

First Edition: August 2023

About the Author

She had always wanted to be a writer since she was a child. While she chose her path in life, studying literature and linguistics was the first step towards her goal. Meanwhile, she kept working as a copywriter for her college magazine to keep up the rhythm. Time flew by, and she graduated to begin her work as an instructional designer at one of the Big 4 firms. Her job entailed juggling multiple tangents of media, content, and graphics. She felt as though she belonged there because her profession was nothing short of a fantasy that she had always wanted to live. She got to script, design, and suggest ideas that would make a difference in the project's delivery. And not just that, she was slaying her professional front; her family has always supported her in pursuing her dream of being a writer. Today, as you read these words, she is an author, a happy corporate professional, and a fiercely independent individual who will pursue her aspirations regardless of life's difficulties.

Thanks to Bublu and Tainu for being so patient and supportive.

Editor's Note

When I first had the privilege of reading the book, I was immediately captivated by the unique blend of narrative storytelling and poetic elements that permeated its pages. Juri's writing style, characterized by descriptive language and a profound ability to paint vivid pictures, creates an immersive and engaging atmosphere that draws readers in from the very beginning.

As I delved into the first part of the text, centered around the theme of mothers, I found myself deeply moved by her portrayal of the universal love and admiration we hold for these remarkable individuals. Through relatable phrases and sentiments, she masterfully captures the essence of maternal love, skillfully comparing it to the nurturing forces of nature. The language flows effortlessly, enhancing the emotional impact of the piece and evoking a profound sense of connection with the sentiments expressed.

The narrative then takes an intriguing turn as it follows the journey of Diya and her path into motherhood. Here, Juri employs a more structured narrative approach, using dialogue and vivid descriptions to bring the characters to life. I found myself drawn into the story, witnessing firsthand the experiences and emotions that unfolded. Themes such as intuition, love, and independence are seamlessly woven into the narrative, adding layers of depth and authenticity to the storytelling.

The book takes a subtle shift in tone as we enter the second part, where a more introspective and reflective atmosphere emerges. She skillfully contrasts expectations and realities within relationships, delving into the complexities of communication and the yearning for genuine connection. Through the use of poetic verses, she explores the depths of longing, the sting of disappointment, and the transformative power of self-realization. It is through these heartfelt expressions that readers are invited to contemplate their own experiences and emotions.

Throughout the book, Juri consistently demonstrates a profound command of language. The skillful incorporation of descriptive imagery, metaphors, and relatable themes serves to heighten the emotional impact of the words on the page. The transitions between narrative and introspective moments are executed with seamless precision, maintaining the reader's interest and capturing the essence of the characters' journeys.

This book is an exceptional work that seamlessly combines narrative storytelling and poetic elements. Its unique style and Juri's ability to convey depth of emotion through language make it a truly captivating read. As you embark on this literary journey, I encourage you to immerse yourself fully in the words and allow them to evoke a myriad of emotions within you. May the stories and verses within these pages resonate deeply, offering solace, insight, and inspiration along your own personal journey.

Table of Contents

Childhood!

I want to relive my childhood again,

where I don't have to wait for life's train.

I could happily cycle inside my house,

and not worry about travelling solo to a lighthouse.

I want to be a juvenile once again,

where I cry for all the silly reasons.

Yet I don't have to justify the grounds,

for all the trauma caused by emotional pain.

I want to get back to my days of babyhood

because I don't have to breathe with the fear of being misunderstood.

Curating emotions based on others' convenience,

is not a mandatory ritual you have to follow to maintain the sequence.

I want to relive my childhood again,

where the world is my stage, and I am the only conqueror.

I could be rebellious and demanding together,

Yet I won't be judged enough to sustain.

Maa!

'Raising you alone was like raising ten kids'

My friends say they have heard this sentence before.

The reason could be that it's every household's common verse,

Making our moms one of the lovable beings in the universe.

As birds leave their nest while they grow up,

we astray and make our world as a matured human cub!

She still never forgets to check on her kids,

no matter how old they grow, even in their hundreds.

Addressing her is the first word every child utters,

as she will always act as nectar while they suffer!

'Maa' is a word beyond emotions can ever reach,

I can't get enough of her, it's way beyond what I can preach.

Mothers are nature's best creation, not sure who exactly quoted it but whoever did could really understand that mother nature has always been a giver, and she created moms because she knew she can't be present everywhere all the time. And while she's busy juggling her responsibilities, she wanted our moms to nurture us like no other. And while she shared that responsibility, she also guided the moms in every step of their life to experience the love and attachment a new soul has to offer. This responsibility is not easy; she needed a warrior to take up those duties, but she wasn't looking for someone super perfect. She wanted that warrior to explore the challenges and find her way through them with patience.

Diya was in her 8th month of pregnancy, while she was going to the office one day, she was feeling that her baby moved inside her a lot that day than usual. This was her first pregnancy, and she didn't know what to expect, curiosity piqued in, and she browsed the internet to see if she was alright before consulting a doctor. She read that as she gets closer to her delivery date, it's quite normal as the baby grows the space lessens inside the womb. She finished her day; Shiva her husband came to pick her up and they went to the gynecologist to ensure it. The doctor agreed and cautioned Diya against spending a lot of time online researching pregnancy-related information because most of it might not be accurate.

A month later, she delivered a beautiful princess. They named her Freya, Shiva and Diya were so excited about their kid that they decided on the baby names while they were 6 months through their pregnancy.

A few names for a girl child and a few for a boy, but somehow their intuition said that it was going to be a girl. And their intuition wasn't wrong; Freya came with so much love in her life that she was extremely adored by everyone around her. Diya thought motherhood was difficult, but with Freya around her, she was amazed to see how easy she makes it for her to be a mother.

Not just that, Shiva has been an amazing husband and a father throughout - a guy who has mastered patience to a level which comes across as nirvana to people.

Freya is addictive and infectious. With both working parents around her, she has learnt to be an independent baby, like all other covid babies these days. She understands her parents right from her babyhood and considers her parents as her role models.

<u>Mother nature chose her warrior without second thoughts and her warrior Diya was excelling at it, she took this responsibility as an accolade, a beautiful ornament she wouldn't ever give up on.</u>

Experiences!

Four hours and thirty minutes delayed,

a few hours before her solo trip, she was notified!

Some notifications make you anxious,

Yet experiences are only filling her life's empty canvas.

She takes small sips of a cup of coffee and wanders,

this long wait for her flight will make her go bonkers.

Suddenly, she thought about what this place has to offer,

Don't airports have a lot of stories to share?

A man hugging his mom while she departs,

A couple holding their hands while they travel together,

A girl looking for a charging point as she ran out of charge on her phone,

A solo traveler taking her first solo trip while her flight is delayed.

She can't help but be glad about the encounters witnessed,

With her flight on time, will these details add value to her bewilderedness?

She wants to take a chance, should she?

She was on the verge of pouring her soul,

When his thoughts took a stroll!

Bewildered, she took a step back, to think,

Why for once can't she let her heart sink?

Why is it so difficult to trust a stranger?

Do they only intend to break hearts?

If cautious steps make the journey mundane,

Accelerated approaches mostly put one in pain!

She reckons 'true love' is an utopia,

Realizing that the very first steps towards it start with 'trust'.

Surprises are always a part of unexplored voyages,

If Cinderella won't lose her shoe that night,

She wouldn't find her knight in shining armor, right?

Power Dad!

Why do you treat me like a kid, daddy?

questions a matured millennial in anxiety.

His dad rolls his eyes, and looks at him with a faint smile,

thinking 'He has physically grown but still acts infantile.'

Some questions are rhetorical, says his father,

but I would still have an insightful answer, which you wouldn't prefer.

If all the rules were meant to be broken,

I would pretend to be your son for a day!

'How does that help, Dad?' He asked!

I think you are trying to twist my question.

Father said, 'When his son likes the way his dad cooks,

when he can't wait for his dad to arrange his messy house,

when he expects him to clean his white shoes, which went grey.

I am not sure if millennials should raise such interrogations.'

Don't tell me that you miss me!

Don't tell me that you miss me,

When you can't spend a pulse for me!

Thy words take me to a world of fantasy,

where fondness doesn't come as anarchy!

Don't tell me that you think of me,

When you can't spend a moment with me.

Flattery uttered with a smile is always masked with a lie,

And I have fallen bait to everything which I can't deny!

Don't tell me that I mean something to you,

When you take every next step only after I do.

Pouring chivalry in my presence is a trait,

And making me redundant in my physical absence can't be taken straight.

Don't tell me that you want to explore territories with me,

When your actions speak louder than your words for me!

Sweet talks make my heart ponder,

concluding that I found the one!

Only to realize that you are a mirage,

silently crept in, to make my mind wander!

Deanna and Jovi were childhood friends, went to the same school and parted during their higher studies. The unspoken bond remained but none of them expressed what they felt for each other, and time flew from days to months to years. Their new chapter as corporate professionals started, and while both of them were aggressively trying to achieve the best in their careers, destiny planned to have both of them placed in the same city. They were in different companies, while he was a management consultant, she was a software engineer, but they were unaware of the fact that a new chapter is about to begin.

Deanna went out partying one night partying with her colleagues, she saw someone who looked like Jovi but ignored thinking she might be too tipsy to recognize people, and why would Jovi be in Mumbai? That made her think, where is he exactly now, it's been a couple of years since they last connected. She browses her Instagram and gets surprised to see that Jovi is in Mumbai too. By the time, she was done stalking him, she hears someone say, 'Stop stalking me on Instagram.' That took her by surprise, and she turned back to see who's it and it was Jovi standing right in front of her with a big smile on his face. Deanna couldn't stop hugging him and he reciprocated the same, and then they made plans to meet again.

As planned, they met, and they started hanging out together more often. Jovi would make her the center of the universe when he's around her but would be very unresponsive when he's not around her. He wouldn't call/text her, he would cancel plans abruptly at the last minute and would disappear for days. And he would come back with a sorry every time as if he was playing very hard with Deanna to get him. She was slowly losing patience with him; in a short period, she got so close to him that it was stating to make her feel sad and vulnerable. She was astonished to see Jovi's change in behavior in person and when he was away. She tried telling him that his shift in behavior is creating a trauma, she would want to avoid as she believes communication is the only solution to all the challenges around. Jovi found this very silly and said I like you, but I don't have to prove that every day to you, I need my space and I give you attention in person, don't you see that?

Deanna had nothing to say in return, she said 'Sure, Jovi', and took a decision. What did she do next?

Unmasked Feelings!

Unexpressed emotions are precious,

They hold spacious feelings!

Capturing a huge fragment of your heart!

Stitching those feelings with your priorities,

Could be a piece of art!

Nascent stages are a blessing,

holding on to more than you should,

Within prevails the excitement of confessing and messing!

Adoration doesn't come with boundaries...

With every passing day, they will keep growing strong,

And with them by your side, things can barely go wrong.

Missing the presence of that person can be weary!

With a contentment that this distance is just temporary.

Being drowned in emotions may lead to a saccharine rush...

Especially when you want to be an open book of romance...

Failed only to be stronger!

When the world was crashing down at my feet,

I couldn't find a human who would walk with me on the street.

I didn't seek a companion who would take a stab for me,

Albeit I kept waiting for someone who would enjoy silence by the sea.

'Expectations hurt' is one of the most overrated phrases,

A golden rule to be set before any journey starts.

Stumbled upon the same 'expectation' stone with a vision very hazed,

fell so hard this time, that I couldn't measure the blaze.

Only to realize not all falls lead to failures,

like the phoenix who rose from the ashes.

Not to prove the worth it pertained,

but for itself to show that, if not pleasantries, with fire it can sustain.

Daughter: A dream!

Chubby cheeks, tiny nose, dimpled chin, golden curls,

The addition of five tiny fingers and toes increased the family by a few yards.

They dreamt of a little fairy to fill their lives with merriment,

And there she came with a bundle of happiness to fulfil their present!

Sleepless nights didn't feel like a nightmare,

Baby's cooing sound felt like a dream wear,

Those soft kicks with her cute legs rose higher,

As if they were an embodiment of something she wants to conquer!

Her smile made the world go weak on its knees,

Cuteness would attract hands on her cheeks to squeeze!

Turning pink with a smirk, she would start to giggle,

A melody would cover the entire house leaving it rhythmical.

Beloved, are you real?

This time,

She didn't have to pretend to be happy,

As there's almost nothing around her

that makes her unhappy!

She met him for the second time after months,

Finally, destiny conspired to bind them together as they confront!

This lad made situations very simple for her,

held her hand when anxiety would kick in,

and her vision would blur.

He knew she was strong from the outside but needed nurturing,

with every frown of hers, he would shower attention without thinking!

She would look at him and be at a loss for words,

His charisma and chivalry with a layer of empathy aren't any less!

A reader she was, always thought that fiction is more beautiful than reality,

yet she wakes up every day to anticipate that having him as her eels like a fictionality.

Grave Loss!

Can you hear me out from the skies?
Where dreams are extra-terrestrial!
I have been wanting to pass on my thoughts,
But reaching you at the other side is like detangling a jumbled knot.

I saw you on a summer evening, at the golden hour,
Could feel an upsurge of emotions landed on me like a meteor shower!
You were satirical in your expressions,
And with every passing day, I couldn't help my obsessions.

Days passed, and I was taking a deep dive into the ocean of love,
Only enamored to know, you echoed the same as a beloved!
Overwhelmed, I took a moment and thought to confess,
Little did I know that it won't be a success!

My phone rang, 'He left for heavenly abode, this morning!' a voice uttered.
Am I dreaming, or I am in a state of hypnosis-my consciousness muttered!
My profound emotions were streaming down the lanes of sorrow,
Wish I followed my heart rather than my mind, I couldn't wait for tomorrow.

Love never came easily to him, he found it in places and situations he expected it the least. There came a point where he thought he was not meant for love, and all the novels he read, the movies he watched, and the stories he had heard are nothing but a utopian concept. Then he met a girl through a dating app, they started chatting around 9 a.m. after they matched, and she asked him if he could meet her in the evening once he gets free from the office. He thought to himself that never in his life has his energies synced with sometimes within hours and he doesn't want to delay it any further, and with that thought he decided to meet her. They met at a coffee place and their conversations had no end, and being on the first date they planned their second. The second date, he asked her out for dinner, and he had to wait a bit for her as she ran a little late. She came after a while, and he couldn't stop looking at her as looked like a moon making others redundant. That date was special, they both skipped their heartbeats together and went back home very content. A few days later he called her to see a few of his friends, she joined him, and she behaved in a way as if she always belonged there. He wanted to let her know that he has fallen for her, and he thinks he found the one at the oddest of times when he was about to give up on love. He took her out on a drive, and while he was on the verge of letting him know about his feelings, she stopped him and said...Yash, I have something to say, and said that she's unwell and he needs to know. Yash took it very lightly and said, we all fall sick and recover, so will you. She unraveled the story by adding that her both kidneys have failed and she's undergoing dialysis. She also added that this is fatal, and she has no visibility into her future.

It got a bit much for him to digest, but he still expressed his feelings for her. She was in tears when she confessed that she felt the same, but it would be unfair for her to give him hope at this juncture of her life. He replied that love means sticking through thick and thin, and he would want to be there for her. She said she would let him know. They kept on meeting at regular intervals, and slowly her health started to deteriorate; he even accompanied her to the hospital with the hope that she would accept his proposal and be his girl someday. Months passed, she slowly started to recover, and it was December 30, almost the new year. That night she met him and said, Yash, I decided to be with you; you make me weak on my knees. Yash was in seventh heaven; they spent some quality time together and headed back home. The next morning, he didn't hear from her, unlike other days. He kept on calling her, but she was unresponsive. He gets a call from her number, and there's someone else at the end stating, 'Rumi passed away last night with a cardiac arrest.' His world came crashing down; he couldn't see things clearly as his eyesight was blocked by tears.

Yash was devastated; will he believe in love again?

Does it exist?

Love is limited to books and verses, that's true,

Investing time in knowing someone is tedious,
And we are scared to invest a lot more than commit,
Explicitly sour yet so challenging to admit.

They are together for decades, as they claim,
but why is posting pictures on Instagram the only aim?
Billion-dollar smiles to pose while holding hands,
yet strangers sitting together, for the attention phone demands.

Where do people find those tickling love butterflies?
Does gestures still go a long way as they are portrayed?
Conversations are a luxury, without content it all feels shallow,
But enjoying silence is someone's presence, is the love I wish to follow.

Emotional bliss!

Lost in the maddening crowd, she could hear a whisper,

which awakened the soul deep inside with a picture.

Reckoned the divine feeling of love was traumatizing,

comprehended—being in love with 'him' will make pain only a 'luxury.'

She dreamt that night, "What's love," he asked.

Knowing her feelings couldn't be masked.

It is the thought of you when the first ray of light settles in my eyes, she replied.

Enveloped in imagination, she woke up!

Sailing in adoration, she thought! Bounded to you my 'emotional bliss',

I feel so flamboyant despite being alarmed.

If promises were not meant to be broken,

I would vow this eternity for you.

Oh, Flower!

Blooming flowers secrete particles of ecstasy,

Leaving the world to drown in fantasy!

Let's not question the purpose of its survival,

Beauty to the beholder doesn't come with denial.

Are these the colors of the rainbow, they borrow?

Or these are the heavenly colors the Omnipresent sparkled on them?

Were they supposed to have one color throughout their span of existence?

Or were meant to bloom, only to make others happy?

Nevertheless, her entity is linked to an unsought purpose.

She is a piece of the spiritual realm in a holy shrine.

Sometimes a bunch of emotions bind a ritual.

Spectacularly standing out without public validation.

Will always be a composition to rejoice,

Alternatively, an untouched emotion left for Joyce.

Miss Sassy!

She's my company when I seek solitude,

I want to be alone but can't help her attitude!

Shooed her away a few times but she's adamant,

She would still fly in with her beautiful feathers any moment.

Who's this pretty, who she senses my loneliness?

Occasionally checks on me which feels a little nosy.

Yet she's is on a mission to be my constant companion,

Hence, she laid two eggs in an empty vase amidst my plantations.

Miss Pigeon, why did you place your trust in me?

Can you trust your babies around me?

Maybe they trust their intuitions about a person,

they know that being tough from the outside for a person, is not their only version.

Wondering did she decipher my empathy behind my arrogance?

My growing adoration for her behind my avoidance?

Did she know I longed for her while she was away?

Did she find a reason to be my companion and stay?

Summers can be really exhausting, it's time for her to make a nest so that she can lay her eggs and keep her babies safe. Humans have been really hard on her off late, someone did spread a rumor that pigeons spread diseases and it is not a very positive experience for her lately. Otherwise, she would just hop onto someone's balcony and lay her eggs. But life starts when one steps of his/her comfort zone, so did for her. She flew long that day, and while she was looking for a home for her babies to grow, one balcony in a high-rise society caught her attention. A girl was standing alone there lost in her thoughts, she seemed a bit sad, it appeared to her that she might stay alone otherwise where do you see humans sulking alone these days? Anyway, why would the pigeon care, she was on a mission, and nothing can divert her now.

She kept on looking for her abode for almost a week now, and every evening she would see that girl standing on the balcony, wondering something. Miss Pigeon was almost attaining motherhood, and she thought to herself, the lone girl on the balcony needs someone, and I want to be there for her as a companion. Somewhere deep inside her, motherhood chimed in. She decided to fly there the next day, exactly at the time she saw the girl, and she did. She landed on her balcony, and she quickly ran a scan on the balcony to check the surroundings. What caught her attention was the empty vase in the corner. She thought it was a sign from the universe; this is the perfect place for her to lay eggs. Then she made her move and sat on the empty vase. The sulking girl gave her a vicious look and tried to shoo her away. The pigeon got scared and flew back to her base. She was adventurous and nurturing; she wanted to lay her eggs there at any cost, and she didn't want the girl to be alone anymore. She flew there again, and the girl kept pushing her away. It was during one of those days when the girl was crying, and she didn't shoo away the pigeon anymore. The pigeon was very adamant; she didn't want to leave her alone anyway, not least after she saw her crying alone.

The next day, the pigeon notices that the girl left some food and water on the balcony, and this moves the pigeon. She decided to stay there, and she finally laid her eggs. Days passed, and the girl started talking to her. The pigeon got to listen to her at length about her stories and how her days were passing. The pigeon has developed an unseen bond with her; she felt so safe that when the eggs hatched into two beautiful babies, she would leave them alone with the girl and enjoy her 'me' time. The babies would litter the vase, but the girl got some clothes and transferred the babies on them so that they would stay warm and cosy, and she would change the clothes every fourth day. The girl wasn't lonely anymore; she was a part of a family she wouldn't want to give up on. The pigeon thought, now she's a mother to her two babies and a lone human.

Like they say, happiness can be found in the most unexpected places; all you need to do is just believe.

The Sky and the Sea!

It's a gloomy day today and I want to be engrossed in depth,

is the sky conspiring to rain while it's trying hard to not to poureth.

We speak to our peers while we sync in sorrow,

Does the sky feel lonely as it stands strong upon us and a bit hollow?

Imaginations kept crashing my mind as the waves crash the shore,

walking on the beach is one of the experiences I fancy to the core.

I am still deciphering who's the companion to the sky,

Maybe this walk on the beach will help me discover the 'who' and the 'why'?

But seas always add fuel to the deeper thoughts,

the blue bodies calmer on the outside yet rumbling against nature's knots.

Now while my thoughts take a dip, I see that the sea is a tad lonely too,

Seeking a companion, it always takes objects from the shore with a woo.

While I try to reach the end of the sea as far as my vision reaches,

where the blues are merged, and they no longer look lone or distant.

Each drenching in each other's company yet not trying to escape,

Making fairytale love stories a beautiful part of the earthscape.

Dear stranger!

Hope this poem finds you in your solace...

While you wait for your dearly beloved!

Sonnets penned by Shakespeare are a cliche...

But the restlessness to know a stranger is pioneering!

A simple walk led to those fleeting memories,

And the mental blocks saw a new ray through the window of hope!

To escape from the daily clutter...

To not be a lover or a partner.

But to seek you as the piece of heartfelt charm.

Mirror!

Opening his eyes, he would straight away head to the mirror,

the first glance of self-love will only make his aspirations bigger.

He doesn't need others to pat his back while he succeeds,

as he has learnt to be his own cheerleader, as he proceeds.

The mirror that stands in that beautiful corner is his true mate,

with it began his journey to accept his beautiful scars without blaming his fate.

He is falling in love with himself and has a boost in his confidence,

he realized his true strengths and doesn't seek the need for worldly dominance.

He sees his surroundings with a contentment in his heart,

as he feels that finding beauty in imperfections is an art.

Later than never, he discovered his worth which for him was a myth,

the journey onwards and upwards began, and limit is beyond zenith.

Raised amidst a family of models, Keev was a bit skeptical about his looks. He was a good-looking healthy lad, but his family would ask him to tone up as they considered a lean figure would complement his persona more. That notion created a sense of self-doubt in him and that grew stronger with time. He felt he doesn't fit in, and his confidence dropped with time so much that he almost stopped introducing himself to the world that he belonged to a camera-facing family. He had a fear in him thinking what if he gets lost in the societal norms and remains anonymous?

Keev aspired to do something different, something not his family does as he never enjoyed the limelight and was a camera-shy person. He wanted to be a corporate slave, where people love to get glued to their 9-6 routine and they come home to their homes at a time where someone is waiting for them at home to eat food together. He wanted to go grocery shopping on weekends and do laundry as weekends are the only rescue for corporate professionals apart from public holidays. All in all, he wanted to lead a simple life where he didn't have to care about his public appearance as his family demands.

He was reading an article on one of those days where he read about one of the plus-size models and her story from being overweight to absolutely rocking it on the stage moved him. She narrated in her article how hard it was to break through the stereotypes of modelling and get on a stage to be appreciated by the masses. She showcased that self-love is so underrated that while we seek constant validation from the world, in that process we keep on losing a part of ourselves that will be drowned in eternity. She was no different from the rest, she wasn't self-aware then, there was a time when she only was insecure of her flaws, but those flaws were her wings to heaven later. Though late, she focused on making those flaws her strength and tried to love herself rather than waiting for someone else to fall in love with her and make her feel ecstatic. And when that trajectory shift in her mindset happened, she stood firmly in front of the mirror. She witnessed an angel who's not only beautiful but extremely powerful, her scars shinned like the stars in the sky, her confidence swiftly rocketed and there was no come back after that.

Reading all that, Keev had a soul-awakening realization he felt like he woke up from a beautiful dream. As if he never wanted to be scared, insecure, or submissive to the world about what they must think about him after all. What did he do next, did he leave behind his fears and live his life in a way he always thought of?

Ray of Hope!

She knew the warmth in her heart this time wasn't usual,

Took moments to realize that the bursts of emotions aren't casual.

She found a new ray of hope amidst challenges,

Felt blessed to reckon that he was the one turning those challenges into passages!

Luck never favored her when she wanted to blossom in love,

a giver she was who would fit like a glove.

Left her wandering how far she can push her boundaries,

for strangers who used her as mere supplementaries.

Rebellious in nature, once again she was ready to set her heart on fire,

taking another stab, she wanted to fulfill her unfulfilled desire.

She felt a positive aura around him, which filled her heart,

without words he made her feel that he wanted to be a part!

How could she let go this musician who would only hit the right chords?

He was healing something he didn't damage, with efforts.

She started to listen to the words he would utter through his eyes,

his gestures didn't just pierce her soul but came as a beautiful surprise.

Travelling Solo!

Adventures always tickled his mind,

but turning them into reality turned him blind.

Was it his overthinking nature or was he scared?

The fears were overpowering more than he dared!

Sipping on a coffee with friends, his eyes caught her attention,

She was alone and carefree, playing games with obsession.

He never saw anyone enjoying one's company so lavishly,

She caught him staring at her and looked back viciously.

That night, he wanted to step out of the box, he created,

A box which revolved around his comfort zone, as it expanded.

His baby steps led him to his laptop to browse,

'How to enjoy your own company while you stay away from your house?'

The internet did a throw a lot of options on his face,

overwhelmed again, he wanted to shut her down!

But this time something came across as a self-awakening,

And he knew solo travels will lead him to the path of discovering!

Single child Joel was always the apple of his parents' eyes. The attention he would get is inevitable, as his parents dreamed of him for a long time, and he has filled the void lingering around for years. They wouldn't leave him unattended for a moment, and as working parents, it initially became difficult for them to manage their schedule smoothly. Hence, his mom decided to give up her job and shower him with all the love and care he deserved. Joel slowly turned into a teen when he started hanging out with his friends, and during those hangouts, his mom would be worried, and she would call him an endless number of times to check if he was having fun, if he had food, if he needed to be picked up, and if he could keep her updated about every moment. His friends would make fun of him, stating that he's still a kid and needs to be babysat. But Joel loved his mom; he reckons the sacrifices she made prioritized him over everything and everyone. While he had nothing to complain about, he sometimes fancied how carefree his friends' parents were, as they would let them do anything they would wish to, and that's when his friend Robi said that he was going on a solo trip to Ladakh. Joel had his eyebrows raised with curiosity to know more about the trip, how he planned it, how he could dare to go solo, isn't he scared, and what his parents had to say. Robi said that if you are really interested, let's meet up before I leave for my trip, and we will discuss things in detail so that you can plan your first trip soon. Another friend chimed in then and said, "I would like to join you both, as I am on the verge of booking my tickets and staying for my solo trip, and

Robi, I wouldn't mind a bit of knowledge transfer from you.

The day ended, and he couldn't stop explaining to his parents what an interesting meeting it was with his friends today as they were planning trips.

His parents said, solo trips are not for everyone and Joel, you have not stayed alone even for a night, we hope you are not planning anything so adventurous at this age, as you have a lot of time in the future to kickstart your trips and we wouldn't bother you then as you will be on your own. For now, just concentrate on your studies and rest will fall in place. His parents supported his interest, but they were just a little mindful. Joel understood that his parents care, so he parked his interest for a few years later. A few days later he met his friends and while they discussed the idea of travelling solo all over again, he realized he had his heart racing because he wanted to explore those unknown territories too. Those conversations ignited a fire in him, and he wanted to venture out on a journey unknown.

So, did Joel plan his trip, if he did who/what was his inspiration?

A painter who painted her RED!

Colourful life yet the red colour was significantly missing,

She wondered what it would be to have hues of red amidst diverse colours!

While she stood on the balcony one day, she looked at the sky in bewilderment,

Deciphering why did the first rain post-summer, kiss her face in endearment?

Cupid played his cards well, and cast a magical spell,

A painter entered her life with a bagful of colours to get her out of her shell.

She said, 'Oh painter! Can you spot the missing colours in this canvas?'

He silently took out his brush and focused on increasing the brightness!

With every stroke of his brush, he painted all the gaps red!

The bright shadow emitted light up the entire picture; witnessing that she froze like a dead!

Red is the colour of love, belief, and trust, he said!

And no canvas can shine brighter without redacting as a thread!

A thread that binds everything together from dusk to dawn,

A thread that stitches broken hearts recovering from the saga of heartbreaks!

Every time someone finds their life fulfilling yet incomplete,

Universe will secretly send a painter to seal the cracks with love without being discrete.

Marvel, my Pup!

A winter night a forty-day old puppy stood shivering,

all alone, trying to stand straight; he was whimpering.

Stopping my car, I went close to him with skepticism,

he looked at me the way I look at my parents with nativism.

Without holding back, I picked him up with affection,

a mother in me grew, who would hold her baby with protection.

'Marvel' was the first word that hit my mind after finding him,

and taking him along that night was a mission, I wanted to accomplish.

I couldn't imagine a tiny creature will have so much love to offer,

and I can only reciprocate the same or only more as a barter.

Those chubby paws promise me that he has come to stick around,

with a bag full of sweet moments, and endearment to surround.

Have I found a baby in a puppy; I can't stop obsessing over?

With a possessive mother, making choices for the baby being only bolder!

Getting a dog after what happened the last time, she couldn't imagine it in her weirdest of dreams. And it's true when they say dogs need an equal amount of attention as human beings. She felt it when she got **Scoop**, the Labrador, her first dog during her bachelor's. She got him because she needed a dog badly, little did she know that he will teach her to be responsible. He was the perfect epitome of cuteness, but he had also horrified her with a lot of incidents where she was an inch closer to giving up on him. Seema! You lack patience- one sentence she kept on hearing for half of her life yet got Scoop who needed it all in abundance starting patience to love.

It was a monsoon morning in Bangalore, she started her Scooty to go the college; it was drizzling, few miles down the lane a guy came running and bumped into her Scooty. She wanted to save him and with that she had the worst fall of her life. She landed on the ground and couldn't feel her legs, people came running to rescue her. She was immediately taken to the nearest hospital and was admitted. Doctor came after a while and said, you have three fractures on your right leg. She was distorted in her mind thinking how is she going to manage herself and Scoop? She came home trembling in pain, Scoop came running too and all she could do is hold him and cry as much as she could. As if her world fell apart that day and she can't find a way out of it. Poor little Scoop waited the entire day to have her back in the house and play but Seema can't play anymore.

Days passed by and Seema wasn't feeling any better. Her health kind of deteriorated more and it was almost impossible to take care of a puppy who needs undivided attention. A few days later, she was diagnosed with typhoid and Scoop was as usual sitting neglected at the corner of the bed. She cried to sleep that night and thought of finding a home for him, the least she could think of doing for him. The thought of parting from him almost broke her into pieces, she never realized that tiny creature would start to mean the world to her. She called Rhea, her cousin and asked her to look after Scoop. She happily agreed and took him away the next morning stating he will be taken care of as a family member. While Scoop was being taken, Seema could see a certain kind of sadness in Scoop's eyes. As if he was asking her to keep him with the minimal care and attention she could provide. It felt like a baby is being separated from his mother, and Seema felt remorse that she took him away from his biological mother and when he was just starting to get comfortable, he was being given away again. **Is it fair, is life fair, and are circumstances fair; she questioned herself and the universe.** That day something changed in Seema, she felt losing a dog this way is the worst thing that can happen to a dog lover and never in her life twice she would attach herself to a different pet.

A few years later, she saw a puppy on the road, was she still adamant on her decision?

My love for you!

It's not as rosy as it sounds,

It's not as enchanting as witnessing cherry blossoms,

It's not as colorful as the rainbow after rain,

It's not as comforting as guilty pleasures!

Yet it is as calm as the cold breeze on a sunny day;

A gentle whisper amidst loud noises,

It is the missing essence in a perfectly cooked meal.

Yes! It is what we all reckon that we miss.

It may be delayed, albeit,

It will make your wait worthwhile;

Slowly, sneaking in through,

The corridors of your heart to make you smile!

Exactly how I did when it hit my empty shore,

Unexpectedly,

Little did I know that,

all the sweet gestures could overlap collectively!

Music!

Music has healed more souls, therapy could ever heal,

a leap from the reality sometimes feels like a steal.

It has made people cry who failed to express their trauma,

mending broken hearts creating a heartfelt saga.

It has worked as a dedication to express love,

with the finest words one struggles to rise above.

It has been in the form of a lullaby, the mothers sing,

while the baby is put to sleep in a swing.

A loner's best friend while he stargazes from his balcony,

with air pods plugged in acting as his company.

Music has fed his soul with an unending contentment,

so much so that he has found his new form of attachment.

Millennials are busy these days, so was he! It was a corporate job for the world, but he poured his soul out for this job. People often termed him as a 'workaholic', a boy who has devoted himself in entirety to his job. He was often asked 'why does your company make you work so hard that you don't have a life?' Questions as such would irk him to the core, he just wanted to make everyone understand that he doesn't work because he must, he does because he wants to. He is passionate about what he does and if required, he will only go a few extra miles. He would often question himself 'why is it so difficult for people to understand that loving your work is not a myth, it does exist?' And those thoughts would only make him think that it's difficult to convince the world, and if he ever encounters the same question, he will let it go with a faint smile.

He has nothing to complain about in his life, at this juncture. He is a strong, independent man and doesn't necessarily think that he misses out on a companion. A companion to share his day's story, a companion to share his big cup of coffee, a companion to dedicate a few romantic songs, and most of all a companion to hold his hands while he walks on his journey of life. That's also because he has never learnt to complain, he thinks the more you complain, the more you find reasons to be unhappy. It was almost 11 p.m. that night when he finally logged out from his laptop. He wanted to grab some dinner, and then he saw the moon peeping through his balcony door. Looking at the sky has always worked as a therapy for him, so did that night after a long day.

He gets hold of his Air Pods and opens the balcony door. He puts on his favorite song, increases the volume, lights a cigarette and looks at the sky being a little lost. He realizes he is very content in his life, yet he wished he had someone standing next to him and sharing his moments. That could be as minimal as sharing a drag of cigarette or listening to the same song. He smiles in joy and says out loud to the universe:

I know you are there somewhere out there for me,

I am eager to meet you as much as you are!

Old school romance does exist, I feel it,

Here I am keeping the butterflies safe just for you.

Did the universe accept his words? Is there really someone out there for him?

Did she find her muse?

Her circadian rhythm was messed,

Been a few weeks and she can't help wondering what's this feeling of Celeste?

Was a matter to worry but she chose to be cheery!

Thinking why should the thought of the future leave her teary?

A piece of unheard music caught her attention one evening!

Trying to figure out the genre she stumbled upon that feeling!

That music unraveled her artistic soul without any vocal,

Words didn't play a vital role in making her feelings focal!

Was it a utopian reality she wouldn't want to jinx?

Or a mirage she's getting used to as she winks!

She contemplates that miracles often swipe grounds leaving one sleepless!

When reality is better than dreams, she wishes to be dreamless!

Everytime I see you!

The time just stopped as I saw you again,

A flashback of all the time we spent together felt like a series of trains!

The sweat on your forehead shines like a diamond,

And I would want to wipe it off as I am excited!

Excited as that would be a chance to touch your fine-looking face,

A chance I would not want to miss and only embrace!

I can't stop looking at your eyes, as deep as the sea,

So deep that I would like to be drowned in those entering a plea!

While I can't stop obsessing over you, I see sweat running down your cheeks,

Would stealing a kiss right now make me one of the freaks?

Can I confess I haven't witnessed something so pleasant?

With an acceptance in my heart that this is the only constant!

Happy birthday, Stranger!

You passed by...

And my eyes never escaped

You walked into..

With fascinating tales and brave thoughts

Swiped a bit of my ground!

Yet I stayed calm to ponder upon...

what does this stranger hold...

that sets him apart from the world...

And before I squander another moment...

An applause as you are another step closer to your world of perfection!

Here's wishing you a very happy birthday, stranger!